Selected Writings

Selected
Writings

Ruth First

Published in India by LeftWord Books,
in association with partners from
the International Union of Left Publishers in May 2023.

LeftWord Books
2254/2A Shadi Khampur
New Ranjit Nagar
New Delhi 110008
INDIA

LeftWord Books and Vaam Prakashan are imprints of
Naya Rasta Publishers Pvt Ltd.

Cover: Rhuan Oliveira

ISBN   978-93-92018-31-2 (paperback)
          978-93-92018-33-6 (ebook)
'

Printed and bound by Chaman Enterprises, Delhi

Contents

A Note on Attribution

All the essays have been proofread and corrected in accordance with the original publications. Where necessary, the essays have been edited for length.

'Pretoria Conquered by the Women!', protest delivered at Union Buildings, Pretoria, *New Age*, 3 November 1955.

'South Africa Today' *Africa Speaks*, 1961.

'From the Freedom Charter to Armed Struggle', speech at Anti-Apartheid Movement Conference, London 1968.

These three essays are sourced from D. Pinnock, *Voices of Liberation*, Vol. 2: Ruth First, Pretoria: Human Sciences Research Council Publishers, 1997.

'The Limits of Nationalism' is from Part III: An Army for Islam, in Ruth First, *Libya: The Elusive Revolution*, Harmondsworth: Penguin, 1974.

'The Mozambican Miners: A Study in the Export of Labour' (1977), produced at the Centre for African Studies at Eduardo Mondlane University in Maputo, was sourced from the Ruth First Papers project at www.ruthfirstpapers.org.uk.

Introduction

Like Antonio Gramsci, Claudia Jones, Frantz Fanon, Karl Marx, and so many others, Ruth First held multiple roles during the struggles of her time. She was simultaneously a communist militant, a journalist, and a brilliant intellectual. She holds a place of honour in the history of South African journalism and stands alongside its great figures like Sol Plaatje and Govan Mbeki. The gulf between the likes of Ruth First, Mbeki, and Plaatje and the abysmal state of journalism in South Africa today is all too apparent. The same is true, of course, of the gulf between intellectual contributions made in past liberation struggles and the sorry state of intellectual debate in much of our political life today. Moreover, within the academy and outside of it, few contemporary thinkers undertake their work while embedded in a social movement or trade union.

The genuinely radical intellectual always walks a painful path, often stalked by slander, professional isolation, and even exile, imprisonment and murder. Ruth First knew this very well, initially through the experiences of other militants. Steve Biko was murdered in September 1977, and Richard Turner was murdered in January 1978. Four years later, on 17 August 1982, her life too came to a sudden end in the midst of the quotidian act of opening a parcel sent to her university office in Maputo. The letter bomb had been sent on the order of Craig Williamson, a spy for the apartheid state.

The leading African National Congress (ANC) intellectual Pallo Jordan was in the same room as Ruth First when the bomb exploded. The Congolese historian Jacques Depelchin, who was in the neighbouring office, recalled the horror of the scene and how he picked pieces of glass from Jordan's scalp. A few days later, the great jazz pianist Abdullah Ibrahim performed a requiem for Ruth First in Maputo.

In a speech given in honour of Ruth First in 2020, Jordan remarked:

> The full weight of the blow struck against us when the apartheid regime ordered the assassination of Ruth First is felt at moments like the present. Her incisive, analytical mind would have greatly enriched the national debate both inside and outside the liberation movement and helped to define the way forward. Comrade Ruth First was outstanding because she had taken to heart Marx's *Theses of Feuerbach*, where he famously said: 'The philosophers have hitherto only interpreted the world in various ways. The point, however, is to change it.'

Heloise Ruth First was born into a family of communists on 4 May 1925. Her parents, Matilda Levetan and Julius First, were founding members of the Communist Party of South Africa (CPSA), established in 1921. Along with her brother Ronald, she grew up in a household full of lively political discussions with people of different races and class backgrounds. The world outside her home was deeply and violently divided by race, class, and gender, but Ruth was born into a very different home, one in which the full humanity of everyone was assumed. The profound disjuncture between her family life and the world outside instilled a deep commitment to fighting racial, patriarchal, national, and class oppression and exploitation.

Her emancipatory zeal was not solely academic. From a young age, she demonstrated a dedication to both practice and theory, each informing the other. After matriculating from Jeppe High School for Girls, she studied social science at the University of the Witwatersrand. She demonstrated an aptitude for working on various projects in a broad left space. As a student, she served as secretary in the Young Communist League and founded the Federation of Progressive

Students with other anti-apartheid activists. Ruth First's world was miles away from the narrow and often toxic sectarianism that plagues many of the left in South Africa today. Her cohort of fellow students and comrades during this period were a broad swathe of activists, including Nelson Mandela; Eduardo Mondlane, the first leader of FRELIMO; Joe Slovo, the communist lawyer who would later become her husband; and Ismail Meer, editor of the *Indian Views* newspaper.[1]

Ever busy, Ruth First produced a steady stream of writing alongside her political activism and solid organisational work, which appeared in newspapers and journals such as *The Guardian* and *Fighting Talk*. Many pieces, written anonymously by a young Ruth, display her resolute determination to expose the fascist nature of the apartheid state, police brutality and the economic and structural implications of apartheid laws. At the same time, she promoted the non-racial solidarity built up in anti-apartheid organisations through the pass defiance campaign and bus boycotts. Her journalism was not limited to issues of working-class and black people in South Africa. She also held high the achievements of socialism globally. In an article in the November 1948 issue of *The Guardian*, she celebrated the thirty-first anniversary of the formation of the Union of Soviet Socialist Republics (USSR).

After graduation, Ruth First worked as a research assistant in the Social Welfare Division at the Johannesburg City Council. Her tenure there did not last long. She had hoped to be able to deal with the myriad socio-economic problems facing the city. Instead, she was tasked with finding celebratory materials to commemorate the fiftieth anniversary of the city's almanac. The profound contradiction between the sanguine image of Johannesburg presented by the City Council and the reality of Johannesburg could not have been more abhorrent to her.

Throughout the 1940s, it became apparent that the South African racial capitalism system faced a labour crisis. The black unions, growing in strength, began to confront the oppression and

---

[1] FRELIMO: The *Frente de Libertação de Moçambique* or Liberation Front of Mozambique, led Mozambique in the war of national liberation against Portugal which culminated in independence in 1975

exploitation faced by black workers in general and mineworkers in particular. Many of these struggles were led and supported by communists.

By 1944, Prime Minister Jan Smuts realised that the growing agitation by African workers threatened the entire foundations of the South African capital. He put in place more draconian measures to quell the groundswell of protest action and solidarity work. The War Measure No. 1425 issued by Smuts prevented groups of over twenty individuals from gathering on mining property without special permission. However, despite these measures, workers continued to agitate, and by 12 August 1946, thousands of African mineworkers were on strike from the East to the West Rand. As Ruth First noted in 'The Gold of Migrant Labour', published in 1962, 'There is no industry of this size and prosperity that has managed its cheap labour policy so successfully'.

The South African state responded with ruthless violence to destroy the strike. Workers were chased down mineshafts with live ammunition, and there was a vicious crackdown on potential sympathy strikes. Within four days, the state beat over 1,00,000 workers into submission, coercing them back into work. Nine workers were left dead. Many others were arrested and tried for treason and sedition. Among them were trade union leaders, the entire central committee of the Communist Party and many of the ANC leaders based in Johannesburg.

The South African state and white supremacist political parties wasted no time promoting 'swart gevaar' ('black danger') discourse and anti-communist hysteria.

The massacre of striking miners at Marikana in 2012 demonstrated that the South African state across colonial, apartheid and post-apartheid eras has been consistently willing to work for the interests of mining capital and that this has not yet been addressed politically.

Ruth found herself a central actor within the Communist Party as the entire leadership was arrested and detained for their role in the strikes. At this point, she was effectively running the Communist Party's offices and took on the editorship of *The Guardian* while uncovering and reporting the exploitation and oppression of black South Africans. Unlike many communists, she did not have a narrow interest in only struggling against class oppression but understood the intersection between class, race, and gender. She knew that in South Africa, the question of class is also *raced*. These intersections became even more marked in the lead-up to the 1948 elections when the National Party came into power and began to implement the system of apartheid.

In 1949 Ruth First married Joe Slovo. When they met at Wits University, Slovo had just returned from World War Two. Amid their political struggle, they began a family and had three children – Shawn, Gillian, and Robyn. Despite their growing family, First and Slovo never flagged in their commitment to the anti-apartheid struggle and socialism. They also played a leading role in many active and vibrant political campaigns and protests led by the ANC throughout the 1950s.

Her political agitation did not go unnoticed. In 1956, Ruth First was one of the 156 defendants in the Treason Trial that would continue until 1961. Despite being acquitted along with the other 155 defendants, Ruth First was banned in 1960 under the state of emergency imposed after the Sharpeville Massacre. So, despite being acquitted, she could neither attend political meetings, publish any work, nor be quoted publicly.

This attempt to silence Ruth First was not enough for the government, and in 1963 she was imprisoned under the 90-Day Act, making her the first woman in South Africa to be detained under this law. She was jailed without charge for 117 days and was kept in solitary confinement. It was a physically and psychologically taxing experience. Like Winnie Madikizela-Mandela, Ruth First detailed the torturous conditions she suffered in a short but searing book *One Hundred and Seventeen Days: An account of confinement and interrogation under the South African Ninety-Day Detention Law.* It is a classic of prison writing.

After her detention in March 1964, Ruth First went into exile, where she joined the British anti-apartheid movement. In 1972, she became a Research Fellow at the University of Manchester, and a year later, she began lecturing at the University of Durham. Her academic work and political activism remained centred on the African continent.

In 1977, Ruth First moved to Mozambique, where she was appointed professor and research director of the Centre for African Studies at Eduardo Mondlane University in Maputo. Ruth First's Pan-Africanist commitment was clear, and she declared: 'I count myself an African, and there is no cause I hold dearer'. She researched the lives of migrant labourers, particularly those who worked in South African gold mines and then expanded her interests to pioneering work across the African continent. As pointed out by Adekeye Adebajo, Ruth First's work, in the true spirit of Pan-Africanism, rejected the false imperialist dichotomy between sub-Saharan Africa and North Africa. Notably, Ruth First's work did not just look at the impact of Western imperial nations on Africa but also the apartheid state's imperialist ambitions in Southern Africa – through its attacks on the sovereignty of countries, its occupation of South West Africa (now Namibia), and the exploitation of the working classes Africans in neighbouring countries through the migrant labour system. Her commitment to a Pan-African vision was enriched by living in Tanzania and Mozambique.

Most of her work written in the 1970s became ground-breaking within the field of Marxist scholarship. *The Barrel of a Gun: Political Power in Africa and the Coup d'état* (1970), *The South African Connection: Western Investment in Apartheid* (1972; co-authored), *Libya: The Elusive Revolution* (1974) and *The Mozambican Miner: A Study in the Export of Labour* (1977) are excerpted in this collection and display the rigour and innovation of her study. Additionally, *Olive Schreiner: A Biography* (1980), co-written with Anne Scott, evokes Ruth First's lifelong interest in the particular role of women in a patriarchal capitalist society.

Along with so many other radicals from the past, Ruth First has been appropriated into the anodyne liberalism that now dominates significant sectors of South African academics and media. Her communist and Pan-Africanist political orientations are seldom mentioned, and the radical nature of her journalism and work is largely obscured.

Reconstituting a viable left movement in South Africa has to be a future-oriented project rooted in new models appropriate for new times. But Ruth First stands as a model of communist commitment, a bright beacon burning with passion.

Vashna Jagarnath   Johannesburg,
September 2022   South Africa

Pretoria Conquered by the Women!

Johannesburg – In a multiracial demonstration against an unjust law, nearly 2,000 women descended on Pretoria last week and made their way to the Union Buildings to present their protest to four cabinet ministers.[1,2]

Pretoria had never seen anything like it before. Overcoming every obstacle, major and petty, placed in their path, the women came from all parts of South Africa to participate in the demonstration. For hours they poured up the steps of the Union Buildings and congregated in the concourses while their leaders attempted to deliver their protest.

The cabinet ministers ran away from them – so the women left the petition forms on their doorstep to ensure they saw them when they eventually returned to their offices.

[1] [Ed.] The Union Buildings, in Pretoria, are the official seat of the government of South Africa.

[2] [Ed.] In 1955, the South African government declared that African women living in urban townships (segregated peripheral residential areas allocated for Black residents) would be required to buy new entry permits each month. This was a new development of the pass laws – an internal passport system designed to segregate the so-called races, severely limit the movements of the African population, restrict and control urbanisation, and designate officially sanctioned migrant labour. On 27 October 1955, about 2,000 South African women marched to the official seat of the South African government, the Union Buildings, to protest these and other laws that reinforced a racially oppressive society. This mobilisation was a critical step forward in women's organised participation in the anti-apartheid movement as, less than a year later, over 20,000 women would embark on the historic, multiracial anti-pass march to Pretoria on 9 August 1956, now commemorated as Women's Day.

The police resorted to every kind of stratagem to stop the demonstration. The women were banned from holding a meeting or walking in procession. The Transportation Board, at the last minute, refused permits for the buses.

The railways refused the request of the Federation of South African Women for special coaches.[3] When the women presented themselves at ticket offices in the morning, clerks at some stations refused to sell any woman a ticket to Pretoria. Cars were stopped on the roads leading to Pretoria, taxis were ticketed, and large contingents of women were held up at police stations.

But the women were indomitable. They were determined to get to the Union Buildings. And they did!

In all, 1,600 of them converged on Pretoria, sitting for hours outside the Pretoria station while a ferry service of taxis and private cars was organised to take them to the Union Buildings. For hours on the morning of Thursday, 26 October, there was an endless and colourful stream of women, many carrying their children, winding up through the lovely government gardens and to the amphitheatre. There they filled the great granite semi-circle – triumphant that they had arrived, elated as the hours went by and their numbers swelled but calm, disciplined and quiet in their unanimous protest against passes for African women, Bantu education, the Population Register, the Group Areas Act, the Suppression of Communism Act, Criminal Laws Amendment Act, Public Safety Act and all oppressive laws.[4]

[3] [Ed.] Formed in 1954, the Federation of South African Women was a multiracial women's organisation that was part of the wider Congress Alliance, a set of organisations linked to the African National Congress (ANC). The 1956 Women's March was one of the Federation's major achievements.

[4] [Ed.] Bantu Education referred to the inferior education reserved for Africans to secure cheap, unskilled, and semi-skilled labour. In 1950, the Population Registration Act required people to be identified and registered from birth as one of four distinct racial groups: White, Coloured, Bantu (African), and Other (Indian and Asian), whilst the Group Areas Act forced these racial groups to live in segregated areas. In the same year, the Suppression of Communism Act was used to repress organisations that advocated for racial equality, forcing groups like the ANC and the South African Communist Party (SACP) to go underground. In 1953, the Criminal Law Amendment Act and Public Safety Act were passed in response to the Defiance Campaign of 1952, which was a non-violent, mass-based resistance campaign in which protestors performed

From the early hours of the morning, the women began to assemble at arranged meeting places in their townships. They came with their infants, carrying lunch baskets, suitcases and paper carriers; some with blankets, many with huge sunshades. Many found their way blocked at the last minute, but undeterred, they got round the obstacles.

The women of Natalspruit found their buses had been cancelled and drivers of hired trucks threatened with prosecution by the police if they conveyed the women. So the women of Natalspruit set out for Germiston station – a distance of eight miles – and there they bought their tickets to Pretoria.

The women of Orlando were told by the ticket clerk that no tickets would be sold to women. Some found men to buy tickets for them, others persevered, and the clerks resumed selling tickets to all-comers at the end of two hours.

The women of Germiston travelled on a composite train ticket for 307. The women of Brakpan bought a composite ticket for 202. Benoni station refused to sell tickets to Pretoria to women. The people of Alexandra boarded the normal PUTC (Public Utility Transport Corporation) bus for Pretoria. Five miles outside Pretoria, the bus was stopped, directed back to the police station, and held there for two hours. Then the police had to let the bus go. The women of Alexandra arrived at the amphitheatre when the protest was already over, in time to see the last women climbing down the steps. But they got there!

A large number of women from Marabastad in Pretoria were kept in police custody and released only when the protest was already over.

From Bloemfontein, the Free State Congress sent a delegation of five women to take part in the protest. Women came from Klerksdorp and Rustenburg.

One Johannesburg clothing factory closed for the day; the workers were in Pretoria.

Indian women were there in their exquisite saris; Coloured women from the Coloured townships and the factories; a band of

---

acts of defiance and civil disobedience. It garnered international attention.

European women who did sterling work helping with transport arrangements.[5]

An old African woman, half-blind, brought her granddaughter to lead her. African churchwomen were there in their brilliant blue and white; women *dingaka* (herbalists) in their beads and skins with all regalia; smartly dressed and emancipated young factory workers; housewives and mothers; domestic servants and washerwomen; and, holding the delegations together and giving the great gathering that impressive discipline, the women Congress workers who started this protest rolling in the locations and townships some eight weeks ago when the Mother's Congress first resolved on it.[6]

At 10.30 am, the first batches of women were at the foot of the Union Buildings, and the walk towards the amphitheatre started. For two or three hours, there was a steady stream of women winding upwards, and as they reached the amphitheatre, each woman (and there were not many who were not puffing and panting) handed in her signed protest to four women from the four organisations stationed there to receive them.

Then, the women took their seats round the amphitheatre. Throughout, they sat in hushed silence, and the crowd grew more enormous as the morning went by. From the windows and balconies of the Union Buildings the civil service looked on in amazement at this impressive demonstration. The pile of protest forms grew until there were 1,600.

From the cupola, Mrs Helen Joseph, Mrs Lillian Ngoyi, Miss Sophia Williams and Mrs Rahima Moosa announced that they

---

[5] The term 'coloured' was used across the British settler colonies in Africa, as well as South West Africa (now Namibia), to refer to people of mixed race. Although often contested it remains an official term in use by a number of states, including South Africa.

[6] [Ed.] The Congress Alliance was a joint anti-apartheid front formed in 1954, uniting political forces from the ANC, the South African Indian Congress, the South African Coloured People's Congress, the white South African Congress of Democrats, and the South African Congress of Trade Unions (SACTU) into a multi-racial united front known as the Congress Alliance. On 26 June 1955, the Congress Alliance's Congress of the People in Kliptown, Johannesburg, issued its Freedom Charter, collating demands for political and socio-economic rights from anti-apartheid activists around the country.

would deliver the protests to the Ministers. They moved off to a great cry of 'Afrika' and the raised thumb salute. The women went on sitting quietly.[7]

Trailed by reporters and photographers and with the Special Branch never far off, the four went first to the office of Dr Verwoerd, Minister of Native Affairs, who only a week before had told the women his policies were a subject for 'praise, not protest'.[8] The door was locked (it was the lunch hour), so a pile of protests was left on the doormat to await the Minister's return. In the office of the Minister of Justice, a '*niksvermoe-dende meisie*' ('unsuspecting girl' according to *Die Transvaaler*) said with alacrity as the women asked her to hand the protests over to the Minister: "Certainly!"

When the four returned to the amphitheatre and reported that they had delivered the protests, the hush was broken again as the women rose to sing *Nkosi Sikelele* and the sound and harmony rang out from the tiers of women.[9]

Then they filed out of the amphitheatre and down the gardens

[7] [Ed.] Helen Joseph (1905–1902) was a founding member of the South African Congress of Democrats. Lillian Ngoyi (1911–1980), who worked as a machinist at a mine, would become the first woman elected to the ANC executive committee. Sophia Williams-Du Bruyn was a founder of the SACTU. At eighteen, she was the youngest among the leaders of the Women's March. A shop steward for the Cape Town Food and Canning Workers' Union, Rahima Moosa (1922–1993) became involved in the ANC through her earlier work with the Transvaal Indian Congress. She was pregnant at the time of the Women's March.

[8] [Ed.] The Special Branch was the security and intelligence wing of the South African Police. Dubbed the 'Architect of Apartheid', Dr Hendrik Verwoerd (1901–1966) was primarily responsible for conceiving the system of racial oppression that was built via a massive programmeme of rural and urban forced removals to racially segregated areas, racially determined access to jobs and imposing inferior education for blacks. He infamously declared that Africans should have no aspirations beyond being 'hewers of wood and drawers of water.' In 1958, he became the last Prime Minister of the Union of South Africa (1910–1961) withdrawing the country from the British Commonwealth. He led the Afrikaner National Party (NP) until his assassination by Dimitri Tsafendas, an independent communist, in 1966.

[9] [Ed.] Originally composed as a Christian hymn in 1897, *Nkosi Sikelel'iAfrika* (God Bless Africa) was taken up as an anthem of liberation across southern Africa. Versions of the hymn appear in the national anthems of Namibia, South Africa, Tanzania, Zambia, and Zimbabwe amongst others.

on their way home.

No order had been given, and there was no bustle, no confusion, no panic or any hitches. The silent protest was developed by the women themselves. With their dignity, their discipline and their determination, they had carried the day.

South Africa Today

"If you faced our problems, you would act as we do." This is the tenor of the defensive arguments of white South Africans under attack for their country's policies. The conviction that their country has been made the world's whipping boy has given South Africans an injured air. Declarations of the rights of man, of equality of opportunity, preambles to the United Nations Charter, the Universal Declaration of Human Rights, and the successive conventions of the International Labour Organisation are all very well. They might be applicable to other countries, but not to South Africa. On the southern tip of the continent of Africa, runs the argument, is a complex, multiracial society in which western civilisation is at stake.

South Africa regards itself as the beacon of the eternal maintenance of white supremacy on the continent. Governments have come and gone, and parties have been formed and fused in the country's political life, but the policy of white domination has remained constant. The present Nationalist Government is the most extreme advocate of white supremacy government, but its base was laid long before 1948 when it came to power under the premiership of Malan.[1]

Official policy, which governs the relations between the dominant group of three million whites and the majority (nearly ten million) of Africans, is today known as apartheid. Still, in different periods it has

---

[1] [Ed.] D. F. Malan (1874–1959) held the Prime Ministership of South Africa from 1948 to 1954. The South African government began to implement the apartheid policy during these years.

been paraded variously as segregation, trusteeship, the preservation of white civilisation, and separate development. Whether it was segregation or trusteeship in the days of Smuts as premier or the latest modifications in the apartheid policy of the Nationalist Government, all deny the principle or the practice or racial equality in a common society.[2]

That the white man is dominant, there is no doubt. But this, runs the argument, is because he is civilised and superior, not because he is white. A folklore of myths and legends to justify racialism has grown over the years, and the tales vary with the narrator and the audience.

There is the assertion by the whites that they arrived in the southern-most part of the country no later than the first Bantu-speaking immigrants from Central Africa crossed the Limpopo, the northern boundary of the Union, a claim considered important enough for South Africa's representative to make before the United Nations General Assembly. There is the claim that apartheid is the word of God and that racial segregation is specifically enjoined in the Bible. There is the assertion that Africans have contributed nothing to 'civilisation' and that the African, not only in the Union but further afield on the continent, has no history but one lived out in savagery. There is the conviction that Africans are different from the white man in a variety of ways difficult to define. South African obscurantism today under the Nationalists goes so far as to exclude the teaching of evolution in the school syllabus because it poses the unity of mankind. To enforce statutory regulations for apartheid in blood transfusion services so that, regardless of their blood groupings, no white person's life should ever have to be saved by blood drawn from an African donor; and to prohibit autopsies

---

[2] [Ed.] Jan Smuts was a leading soldier, politician, philosopher, and ideologue of white supremacy. A leading figure behind the formation of the British Commonwealth, the League of Nations, and the United Nations. Smuts was involved in the emergence of the post-World War II liberal order, all while crafting segregationist white rule in South Africa. During his time as Prime Minister (1919–1924 and 1939–1948), social unrest prevailed with the Rand Revolt, the Bulhoek Massacre, and the Bondelswarts Rebellion, all of 1921–1922. The National Party was the main political party of Afrikaner nationalism.

on white corpses by African medical men.

Jonathan Swift's inventiveness pales beside South African realities, and indeed it has been said that in the Union, life improves upon satire, though not all the popular legends making up this racial folklore are equally devoid of finesse or subtlety. Yet most variations share the basic concept that the African is different and inferior and that civilisation would be undermined by his admission to its society as an equal.

This argument has two crippling weaknesses. If Africans are inherently inferior, it should surely not be necessary to legislate to keep them so. South Africa's law books bulge with statutes reserving skilled jobs for whites; a special system of Bantu Education has been instituted to ensure that Africans find no place, in the words of the Union's Prime Minister, Dr H.F. Verwoerd, "in the European community above the level of certain forms of labour"; and efforts continue to turn numbers of urban factory workers back into tribalists.

The second weakness in the argument that civilisation would be undermined if the African were admitted as an equal is the unsupported assumption that the African can never come any closer to civilisation – even after generations of the civilising process – as though there were some genetic, immutable quality with which whites only are equipped, and Africans never.

African experience in the Union has been that opportunity has not expanded but shrunk. For instance, as more Africans qualified in the past for the franchise, the qualifications were altered to place the vote further and further beyond their reach until, finally, the African franchise was abolished entirely. It is a scathing reflection on the 'civilising mission' of the whites in southern Africa that after 300 years, Africans are still so backward that they must be totally excluded from sharing in this civilisation lest they pollute it.

Racialism has been an essential factor in the technique of domination in the Union. It has transferred the blame for any backwardness of the African to his own shoulders. The solution to the race problem has been posed primarily as one of breaking down race prejudice gradually over an extended period, long enough both to civilise the primitive and re-educate the civilised in tolerance, and this approach has deflected attention from the main problem. For, above all, racialism has overlaid the nature of domination and exploitation and used coloured prejudice to obscure the techniques of domination. Where privilege can be made to coincide with colour, it becomes far more entrenched and unassailable. And where white skin colour can become the badge of privilege entitling whites to sole entry to skilled trades and professions, granting them the monopoly of political representation and commercial opportunity, one-quarter of the population can be prevailed upon to see the maintenance of 'white civilisation' (or dominance) as the condition for its own continued prosperity and survival.

The presence of several racial groups in the Union has enabled South Africa to plead that her situation is unique and should not be judged by international standards. In reality, though, her problems have been characteristic of those of a country rapidly developing into the industrialised phase, with the accompanying needs of a large labour force divorced from the land and directed into wage labour. Far from being unique, these problems have had their equivalent in many countries, even those with homogeneous populations. In *Caste, Class and Race*, Oliver Cox argues, "As a matter of fact, the white proletariat of early capitalism had to endure burdens of exploitation quite similar to those which many coloured peoples must bear today," and he shows that to justify this treatment, it was argued that the workers were innately degraded and degenerate, and consequently, they merited their condition.[3]

The Enclosure Acts, which forced the peasantry into the mills and factories of newly industrialised England, have their parallel in the Reserve system of the Union, which restricts 70 per cent of the population to 10 per cent of the land. The consequent poverty, together with heavy taxation, impels Africans to work in the white labour areas. Vagrancy laws reminiscent of England during the

---

[3] Cox, Oliver C. *Caste, Class, and Race: A Study in Social Dynamics*. New York, NY: Monthly Review Press, 1959, p. 333.

industrial revolution make unemployment an offence and idleness a sin. The aim of the education system for the poor is to teach them not learning but labour and humility so as to protect the good order of a society which views the efforts of the poor and lowly to emancipate themselves as a threat to its very nature.

South Africa entered the industrial phase only a generation ago and long after earlier developed countries, at a period when the lessons of history were known, and parallel situations might have proved instructive. But racialism has served to blur the similarities and blunt the example, thus not only diverting attention from the basic structure of South Africa's economy, but also concealing the intensity of the exploitation and the excessive rate at which wealth is accumulated regardless of human welfare.

This reality applies, on the whole, as much to the Union's immediate neighbour to the north, the Central African Federation, as it does to South Africa.[4] However, with crude racialism under strong fire from all sides in the twentieth century, both the Union and the Federation have found it necessary to modify its forms, concede here and there to public pressure of enlightened opinion, devise new disguises for the old policies and try to confuse and frustrate African and other opposition.

So, in the Federation, policies that are close cousins to the Union's form of white domination are described as 'partnership' and a new departure in race relations. In the Union, the Nationalist Government, for all its intransigence and contempt for international opinion, has been compelled to try to present its race policies in a more favourable light.

South Africa's all-white governments have made many attempts to refurbish the old house with varying degrees of success. If the Nationalist Government has been able to give the impression to some in the Union that it is moving forwards instead of backward and making concessions where it is really tightening the screw, this

---

[4] [Ed.] The Federation of Rhodesia and Nyasaland, also known as the Central African Federation or CAF (1953–63), was a colonial federation that consisted of three southern African territories: the self-governing British colony of Southern Rhodesia (Zimbabwe) and the British protectorates of Northern Rhodesia (Zambia) and Nyasaland (Malawi).

is largely because white supremacy is rooted in the basic structure of South Africa and has had many long decades to dig itself in.

Since the earliest days of contact, the history of the African people has been one of steady expropriation of their lands, this process being completed and legalised in 1913 with the passing of the first Land Act, which confined millions of Africans to areas too small to support them and their stock. The Union's land policy, linked with taxation, has been the lever, compelling tribesmen to migrate and work in urban areas for low wages. The rapid expansion of gold, diamond, and base-metal mining and the development of industry led to the acceleration of the process. So long as Africans could enjoy the life of subsistence peasants, they could not be pressed into service. Migrant labour has ruined African agriculture by emptying the reserves of able-bodied men for long periods at a times and simultaneously has underwritten the system of low wages. The justification advanced for the policy is that these men are peasant farmers augmenting their rural income by spells of work in mines or towns.

Another important outgrowth of white supremacy was the devolution of segregation through local municipal government. The first Urban Areas act, introduced by the Smuts government in 1923, embodied a principle formulated by a Commission which stated: "The Native should only be allowed to enter the urban areas, which are essentially the white man's creation, when he is willing to enter and to minister to the needs of the white man, and should depart therefrom when he ceases so to minister." Buttressing these main pillars of the segregation or apartheid policy are the scores of secondary supports: the laws enforcing residential segregation and denying Africans freehold tenure in the towns; the denial of technical training to Africans and the closing of doors to the acquisition of skills; the startling disparity between skilled and unskilled wages; the laws controlling freedom of movement which are a vital device in blocking the right of the African worker to bid for work in the best labour markets. The Nationalists have taken over all these basic aspects of the segregation policy but have enforced them more rigidly and with more brutality and thoroughness than any previous government.

Years of enforcing race discrimination against not a minority group but the overwhelming majority of the people of the Union have given white supremacy a new rationale for maintaining itself. There is now the fear of revenge, of the Africans turning on their oppressors, of the rise of a so-called black nationalism against which the whites must defend themselves. The traditional policy of segregation, or apartheid, is the only way, it is now argued with reinforced vigour, to avoid the clashes that must necessarily arise where different races live together.

The African Reserves are to become Bantu National Homes, seven little states in all, with their own representative machinery, commissioners-general to maintain the link with the capital in Pretoria, and tribal ambassadors in the towns to keep urban workers under tribal influence and control. Commissions were appointed to provide the theoretical justification for this setting up of imaginary states within the state of South Africa and to plan for the socio-economic development of the new national homes. Simultaneously the last remnants of African representation in Parliament and the Senate were abolished, and the final threads linking Africans with the general political institutions were cut. From now on, chiefs, tribal authorities and their representatives in towns and country will administer apartheid laws as a so-called restoration of their ancient tribal rights. This is nothing more than a new attempt to modernise methods of indirect rule which have failed colonial administrations in so many parts of the continent.

The Bantustan plan is an ingenious pretext for dealing with Africans as foreigners in their own country, except for the small Reserves to be known as their 'states'. Those African rights which still survive in the towns will be erased, and Africans permitted only as temporary workers on the grounds that they will enjoy full rights in their own areas. But in their own areas, Africans under their chiefs, who hold office only so long as they agree to carry out the line of the Government, will be administered under the laws passed by the Union Parliament and supervised and implemented by the octopus-like Bantu Administration Department which controls

African life in every detail.

Inaugurating one of these tribal authorities, the Prime Minister of the Union told Africans: "The white man also has had his tree of separate development planted a long time ago. Already it has grown big and bears fruit . . .. For progress, the Bantu must also have that tree. They must not be jealous when they look into another man's garden. . .. Tend your own little tree, and it will become big."[5] The hypocrisy of the parable lies in the fact that it was the Africans, as much as anyone else, who tended and continued to tend the white man's tree. And like the Union squatter or sharecropper who farms his inadequate plot only when he has spent the greater part of the year working on his master's land, he must tend his tree only when he has done with the white man's, and then be told is has not flourished like the white man's because he is lazy and his farming methods are backward and outmoded.

The most detailed and far-reaching programme of non-white demands is that of the leading political organisations of the Africans, the ANC, joined by allied Congresses of the Indian people (the South African Indian Congress), the coloured people (the South African Coloured People's Organisation), and the only non-racial trade union federation in the country (the South African Congress of Trade Unions).

The product of these efforts was reflected concisely in the Freedom Charter, which was adopted at an assembly of delegates of all races in June 1955 after a nationwide effort to ascertain the grievances and needs of the common people in all walks of life. This charter is the most radical of the political programmes current in the country and, significantly, forms the central theme of the evidence for the prosecution in the treason trial.

The policy of the Congress movement – the chief drafters of the charter – is based on two essential presumptions closely related to each other. The first is the recognition that with the complete monopoly of government in white hands and an opposition party in decline and handicapped by rigged delimitations and other electoral

---

[5] Duma Nokwe, 'Bantu Areas – Machinery of Oppression', *Liberation*, 30 March 1958.

and constitutional hindrances, it would be little short of a miracle for far-reaching changes in national policy to be achieved through Parliament. The second is the recognition, set out in the preamble to the charter, that "South Africa belongs to all who live in it, black and white, and no government can justly claim authority unless it is based on the will of all the people".

The charter is both a recital of grievance and a declaration of the basic tenets of the Congress movement. The greater part is a claim to rights which have come to be recognised as part of the heritage of every man in the modern age. These include the demands that: The rights of the people shall be the same, regardless of race, colour or sex; no one shall be imprisoned without fair trial; the law shall guarantee to all their right to speak, worship, meet together. All who work shall be free to form trade unions; education should be compulsory, free and equal for all children; adult illiteracy shall be ended by a mass state education plan. The aged, the orphans, the disabled and the sick shall be cared for by the state, fenced locations and ghettoes shall be abolished and laws which break up families repealed. The colour bar in sport and cultural life shall be ended; a preventive health scheme shall be run by the state, and so on through the ten main sections and fifty-six clauses of the charter.

Here there is no concession to the theory that education must be a qualification for the vote, that more 'backward' members of the community must be groomed for civic responsibility before they can be entrusted with it. Here there is no proposal that instead of concerning themselves with the vote, non-whites would concentrate on attaining the more 'urgent' needs of better housing, adequate wages, and social services. Congress policy is emphatic that only political rights are a guarantee against the legislature's continuing to ride roughshod over the interests of the majority of the population. Quite absent from the charter is any suggestion that piecemeal reforms and the repeal of this discriminatory law will be adequate to produce any substantial change in the total situation of discrimination.

How to invert a pattern of three hundred years of white domination? The charter asserts in one of its economic clauses,

"All people shall have the right to trade where they choose, to manufacture and enter all trades, crafts and professions". But a mere proclamation of rights without any corresponding change in the order of things which makes all these fields preserves of whites, gives them little meaning.

Congress is committed to a policy of conquering rural poverty, banishing famine and land shortage, demolishing slums, guaranteeing equal pay for equal work, and ending migrant labour, child labour and contract labour. All these are dependent on breaking the dominant socio-economic pattern in the country. Giant monopolies in the gold mining industry, linked with financial and industrial interests and entrenched farming groups, own and control the national wealth of the country and shape this basic pattern. The charter advocates that, "the national wealth of the country shall be restored to the people, the mineral wealth beneath the soil, the banks, and monopoly industry shall be transferred to the ownership of the people as a whole".

Nationalisation of the basic gold mining industry and monopoly industry, and land redistribution, which are fundamental to the major problem of raising the economic status of the non-white people, are not necessarily synonymous with socialism, and the Congress makes no claim at all to have a socialist programme. It aimed in its charter to reflect the aspirations of all classes and groups in South Africa striving for democratic change. The test for the clauses in the charter was simply: can the programme as a whole be implemented without these, taking into account the nature of the present order?

South Africa's situation is complex because, although the great majority of her people occupy colonial and semi-colonial status, they are not administered by a dominant power from across the seas but by a settled white population in a secure home base within the colonial population and allied with British, American, and other investors beyond her borders. As full and untrammelled independence for any of the newly emerging states of Africa means breaking the ties not only of political but also of financial dependence, so too, freedom for the great majority of the people of the Union means a sharp break with the old subjection in all its forms.

From the Freedom Charter to Armed Struggle

The launching of armed struggle against the South African regime must be seen against the total background: the history of South Africa is one of organised violence applied against the majority of the people. First, the violence of military conquest over three centuries (the last act of armed resistance was the Bambatha Rebellion at the beginning of this century in Natal), and then the institutionalised violence of a political system which entrenches a minority in power against the will and the interests of a majority that outnumbers them four to one.[1] The history of South Africa is also one not of a steady or even gradual devolution towards greater fights for the majority, but of a progressive loss of rights, the abolition of what limited franchise existed as a hangover from Cape liberalism of the nineteenth century, and a consistent undermining and finally abolition of the right of the individual to advance his civil liberties and living standards through the courts and the use of the rule of law, or by political or trade union organisation.

Non-violent protest was a tenet of the Congress movement for the greater part of its history, from the foundation of the African National Congress (ANC) in 1912. The late Chief Luthuli put the

---

[1] [Ed.] The 1906 Bambatha Rebellion was a rural uprising led by Bambatha kaMancinza against British taxation and colonial policy in the province of Natal.

seal on this early period.[2] "Who will deny," he asked in October 1952, "that 30 years of my life have been spent knocking in vain, patiently, moderately and modestly on a closed and barred door? What have been the fruits of moderation? The past 30 years have seen the greatest number of laws restricting our rights and progress until today, we have reached the stage where we have almost no rights at all."

The immediate post-World War II period was a time of great economic hardship for the African people, and also of a great spurt of organisation, in trade unions and mass political movements. But the policy of the Government was to "bleed the unions to death" (the words of a South African Minister of Labour), and to repress the political upsurge. The first years of the Nationalist Government in power were a taste of things to come: there was a great spurt of repressive legislation from the all-White Parliament and one after another the few remaining rights of the Non-White people came under attack. The legislative record of the Nationalist Government has been well documented elsewhere. So, too, has the growth in strength and influence of the resistance movement, that mustered great national protest strikes and an impressively disciplined Defiance Campaign against Unjust Laws during which 8,500 volunteers courted imprisonment in order to draw attention to the seething bitterness of the Non-White people and the urgency of their claim.

The campaigns of the fifties were the years of mass mobilisation of the Africans, the Indian people and the Coloureds, with the support of a small sprinkling of anti-racial Whites, and also of the hammering out of a programmeme of aims and demands for the liberation movement of South Africa. This latter objective culminated in the Congress of the People, held at Kliptown, outside Johannesburg, on 26 June 1955.[3] The Congress was the climax of

---

[2] [Ed.] Chief Albert Luthuli, Africa's first Nobel Peace Prize Laureate in 1960 and the most widely known and respected African leader of his era, was President-General of the ANC from December 1952 until his death in 1967.

[3] [Ed.] The Congress of the People was a gathering organised by the Congress Alliance. It aimed to construct a basis for uniting all democratic currents around a common programmeme.

months of organising in villages, factories, mines and townships to get ordinary people to speak out their demands for freedom. They wrote their grievances and their demands in resolutions taken at unknown hundreds of meetings, then elected delegates to come in person to the mass conference that adopted the Freedom Charter. Its demands are well-known, in general:

> South Africa belongs to all who live in it, black and white.
> No government can justly claim authority until it is based on the will of the people.
> The people shall govern.
> All national groups shall have equal rights.
> The land shall be shared among those who work it.
> All shall be equal before the law.
> There shall be work and security.
> The doors of learning shall be opened, and so on.[4]

The Freedom Charter was the first policy document of the mass movement of oppressed people to set out objectives for a non-racial democratic South Africa.

The Government retaliated with the mass arrest of political leaders of all races. Twenty days before Christmas 1956, the Treason Trial opened. One hundred fifty-six political leaders of all races were in the dock. The State charged them with a treasonable conspiracy to overthrow the South African government by violence. The focus of the case was ANC policy from 1952 to 1956, and every document written by or in possession of every one of the 156 was studied minutely and presented as part of the case for prosecution. The trial went on for over four years and eventually collapsed. All 156 were found not guilty and discharged. The State evidence alleging violence had been manufactured. This was the most ignominious defeat of the government in the courts and before the eyes of the world. From then on, the South African government began steadily to circumscribe the powers of the judiciary, to break what independence it had left, and acted beyond the law by edict and

---

[4] *The Freedom Charter*, United Nations Centre Against Apartheid, 1955.

ministerial decree.

While the Treason Trial was still in progress, the country was shaken by the events of Sharpeville in 1960. In March of that year, the police opened fire on mass anti-pass protests in two centres, at Sharpeville in the Transvaal, where 69 were killed and 180 wounded, and at Langa in the Cape, where two died, and 49 were wounded. The ANC called for a national strike as a day of mourning. The government wavered for a moment with its announcement that the pass laws would be suspended, and Chief Luthuli burnt his pass, followed by thousands of others. The government declared a national emergency, and the ANC and the Pan-Africanist Congress were banned. Eighteen hundred political leaders were imprisoned for the duration of the state of emergency.

The following year, 1961, was when White South Africa was preparing to hold a referendum to declare itself a (White) Nationalist Republic. An ad hoc committee of African leaders (that took the initiative because the organisations of the African people were banned) summoned an all-in conference in Pietermaritzburg for March 1961 to draft a non-racial constitution for South Africa and to reinforce its demand that the vote be extended to all without discrimination.[5] The demand was backed by the calling of a national protest strike. The government answered the strike with the country's biggest mobilisation since World War II, as the army and police staged an unprecedented display of armed force to strangle the strike at birth. But for all that, the stay-at-home received solid and massive support throughout the country. It was at this point that Nelson Mandela, who had led the strike from underground, posed the question:

Is it politically correct to continue preaching peace and nonviolence when dealing with a Government whose barbaric practices have brought so much suffering and misery to Africans? ... Have we not closed a chapter on this question?

[5] *Resolutions of the All-In African Conference*, Pietermaritzburg, 25-26 March 1961.

The smashing of the strike – with Saracens [armoured personnel carriers] made in Britain – was the turning point in the political struggle. Africans had decided that the violence of the State made peaceful protest futile.

For the fifties had seen, along with the sharpening of African claims and the maturing of their political organisation, a steady attack on their rights to organise. This started with the Suppression of Communism Act in 1950, which gave the Minister of Justice autocratic power to ban any organisation, newspaper, individual or policy. Bans on trade unionists and political leaders, which were initially for two years, were extended to five. Men and women were restricted to certain magisterial districts, townships and, ultimately, under the 'Sabotage Act of 1962', to their own homes. They were forbidden to enter factories or harbour areas, to attend meetings, to write for publication, to enter newspaper offices, to belong to any organisation which discussed the affairs of the state, to communicate with other banned individuals or be seen in the company of more than one other person, for this was construed as an illegal gathering. Opposition members who had outspokenly expressed their views were sentenced to a state of civil death, and the political movement was drained of its activists for one transgression or another of a myriad of legal restrictions.

From 1953 onwards, the government had empowered itself to suspend all law and rule by decree in a state of emergency. These emergency powers were used not only to crack down after Sharpeville, but also against the peasant revolt in Pondoland, and to this day, Proclamation 400 in the so-called independent Transkei enables the government to detain anybody for any length of time.[6]

The cumulative effect of these draconian laws was to turn South Africa into a full-blooded police state. To organise for political rights,

---

[6] [Ed.] A series of uprisings in what is now the western part of the Eastern Cape province rejecting 'tribal' authorities in the Transkei Bantustan, initiated by the Bantu Authorities Act of 1951. The Bantustan system brought in a hierarchy of 'tribal', district, regional and territorial authorities while increasing the power of certain traditional leaders designated as 'chiefs' who were ultimately subordinated to the apartheid central government. The system increased taxes and reduced popular participation in decision making.

to express political demands, became an act of subversion. Political expression was driven underground, and political organisation was pursued at the peril of victimisation, arrest and imprisonment. It was apparent that for the African people to restrict their opposition to conventional and peaceful methods alone would be to surrender. The more the political organisations proved their ability to rally the African people behind them, the more savage the repression unleashed against them. A dead-end of continuing oppression and discrimination seemed to stretch before the country.

On 16 December 1961, uMkhonto we Sizwe (The Spear of the Nation) emerged with a series of attacks with explosives against government buildings, particularly those connected with the implementation of apartheid, and a manifesto that overnight was pasted on the walls of city buildings:

> The people prefer peaceful methods of change to achieve their aspirations without the bitterness and suffering of civil war. But the peoples' patience is not endless . . . The Government has interpreted the peacefulness of the movement as weakness; the peoples' non-violent policy has been taken as the green light for government violence . . . without any fear of reprisals. uMkhonto we Sizwe marks a break with the past. We are striking out along a new road for the liberation of the people. The government policy of force, repression and violence will no longer be met with non-violent resistance only! . . .

> uMkhonto we Sizwe will be at the front line of the peoples' defence. It will be the fighting arm of the people against the government.[7]

uMkhonto we Sizwe was to complement the actions of the established national liberation movement. The new movement, despite its military character, announced that it did not abandon

---

[7] uMkhonto we Sizwe Command, *Manifesto of the Mkhonto we Sizwe*, 16 December 1961.

the hope and prospect of change without violence in South Africa:

> We of uMkhonto we Sizwe have always sought, as the liberation
> movement has sought, to achieve liberation without bloodshed
> and civil clash. We hope – even at this late hour – that our first
> actions will awaken everyone to a realisation of the disastrous
> political situation to which Nationalist policy is leading. We
> hope that we will bring the government and its supporters to
> their senses before it is too late, so that both the government and
> its policies can be changed before matters reach the desperate
> stage of civil war. We believe our actions to be a blow against
> the Nationalist preparations for civil war and military rule.[8]

So long as there remained the slightest possibility of forcing a
reconsideration of intransigent official policies, uMkhonto we Sizwe
stressed, the armed struggle would remain the supplementary, not
the main form of struggle, and the people would, side by side with
uMkhonto actions, strive as before to find every means at their
disposal to win democratic change by the methods of mass action.

The government answered the formation of uMkhonto we Sizwe
with the 'Sabotage Act', the General Laws Amendment Act of 1962.
It created retrospective offences for which people could receive the
death penalty, it provided for the indefinite detention of political
prisoners – the 90-day Law, which was suspended in January 1965
but replaced some months later by the 180-day detention powers
– and defined sabotage as almost any illegal action taken to further
economic or political changes. Since practically every sort of
political activity was by now unlawful, a trade unionist trespassing
on factory premises or an African taking part in a strike could find
himself accused of sabotage.

The International Commission of Jurists condemned the law
as reducing the liberty of the citizen to a degree not surpassed by
the most extreme dictatorship.

Ninety-day detention inaugurated the official use of torture by

---

[8] uMkhonto we Sizwe Command, *Manifesto of the Mkhonto we Sizwe*, 16
December 1961.

the state. Where solitary confinement did not have the desired effect of manufacturing confessions out of prisoners or forcing them into becoming state witnesses, the Security Police resorted to torture – the statue torture, use of electric shock treatment, and other forms.

The effect of this and other laws was to cram the jails with political prisoners. The wave of repression was nowhere more cruelly administered than in the Eastern Cape, a stronghold of ANC militancy, where, in the space of two years, the Security Police arrested over 1,000 people. Mass arrests, mass trials and the mass dispensation of 'justice' became the order of the day. The State relied for its evidence increasingly on police traps, informers, and the brute extraction of confessions. According to the figures of the Minister of Justice, 3,335 South Africans were detained under various security laws in 1963. According to calculations by a South African newspaper, between March 1963 and August 1964, there were 111 mass political trials in which 1,353 persons were charged. Of these, 44 were sentenced to death and 12 to life imprisonment and 894 to a total of 5,713 years of imprisonment. Among the first casualties of the death penalty for sabotage were Vuyisile Mini, the dockers' leader, and Khayinga and Mkaba, who were hanged in 1964.[9]

On 11 June 1963, the police raided the underground headquarters in Rivonia, a suburb in Johannesburg, and arrested Walter Sisulu, Govan Mbeki, Ahmed Kathrada, and others.[10] The prolonged Rivonia Trial of the nine leaders of the ANC ended in the

[9] [Ed.] Vuyisile Mini (1921–1964) was a trade unionist and uMkhonto we Sizwe militant, later hanged for his role in MK and anti-apartheid resistance in 1964. Wilson Khayinga and Zinakile Mkaba were two prominent ANC leaders who were arrested and hanged alongside Mini, on charges of sabotage and other political crimes.

[10] [Ed.] Walter Sisulu (1912–2003) was an anti-apartheid activist and member of the ANC, serving at times as Secretary-General and Deputy President of the organisation. He was jailed at the Robben Island prison, where he served more than 25 years. Govan Mbeki (1910–2001) was a South African politician, intellectual, military commander and Communist leader who served as the Secretary of uMkhonto we Sizwe at its inception in 1961. Ahmed Mohamed Kathrada (1929–2017) was a Communist and leading militant in the struggle against apartheid. All three were tried for 221 acts of sabotage and conspiracy to overthrow the State.

conviction of life imprisonment of these men, all now on Robben Island. From the dock, Nelson Mandela said:

> I admit I was one of the persons who helped to form uMkhonto we Sizwe. I do not deny that I planned sabotage. I did not plan it in a spirit of recklessness or because I have any love of violence. I planned it as a result of a calm and sober assessment of the political situation that had arisen after many years of tyranny, exploitation and oppression of my people by the Whites.[11]

The events of the early sixties had convinced the African political movement that no possible prospect remained of effecting change in South Africa by peaceful means. Constitutional, parliamentary action has never been open to the African majority. Demonstrations, petitions, massive organisation to prove the representativeness and popular support of the organisations, passive resistance campaigns influenced by Gandhism, uniquely South African-evolved non-violent campaigns, and even the warning shots fired by uMkhonto we Sizwe in its selected sabotage action had left the granite wall policy of apartheid and White supremacy rule unyielding and impregnable.

On 13 August 1967, advance units of uMkhonto we Sizwe, together with fighters of the Zimbabwe African Peoples Union (ZAPU), opened a new chapter of resistance in Southern Africa.[12] Advance units engaged the Rhodesian security forces in fierce fighting at Wankie and other areas. Three pitched battles that month were followed by sporadic engagements, a steady penetration of guerrilla forces into Rhodesia and towards South Africa, and the opening of a second major assault phase from 15 March this year. The South African *Sunday Times* has admitted that "the guerrilla

---

[11] Nelson Mandela, 'I Am Prepared to Die', Statement from the Dock at the Opening of the Defence Case in the Rivonia Trial, Pretoria Supreme Court, 20 April 1964.

[12] [Ed.] The Zimbabwe African People's Union was a Zimbabwean movement that fought against settler colonialism in Rhodesia, from its founding in 1961 until 1980.

campaign is now a full-scale war of attrition".

The Lusaka communique that announced the start of the fighting officially broadcasted the existence of a military alliance between the ANC and ZAPU. This sets a precedent in African resistance, for there is no other instance of freedom fighters drawn from different territories uniting in a common force. Oliver Tambo, ANC Acting President-General, has said that the joint ANC-ZAPU action was to meet the unified strategy of the Unholy Alliance of Vorster-Smith-Salazar:[13]

We are fighting the same enemy ultimately. Our military cooperation flowed from the political cooperation with which we answered the common repression of white minority governments in the South.

[13] [Ed.] B. J. Voster (1915–1983) was the Prime Minister of South Africa from 1966 to 1978 and the fourth State President of South Africa from 1978 to 1979. Ian Smith (1919–2007) was the Prime Minister of the British colony of Southern Rhodesia (now Zimbabwe) an ardent advocate of white rule who, in 1965, declared Rhodesia's independence and its subsequent withdrawal from the British Commonwealth.

The Limits of Nationalism

When in October 1973, Egypt launched the Fourth Arab-Israeli war, it was not Gaddafi, his partner in the projected union between Egypt and Libya, but King Feisal of Saudi Arabia who was privy to that attack plan. It proved to be a limited war with limited goals.[1] Until then, Sadat's policy of trying to cajole the United States into pressuring Israel into acceptable terms had failed; a military success on the battlefield was calculated to induce Nixon and Kissinger to impose a more stable situation in the Middle East. The offensive launched by Egypt, and joined by Syria, was a conventional military confrontation fought by a technically proficient army manned by a generation of university- trained and drafted technicians using textbook tactics.[2]

The Egyptian forces knocked out the Israeli positions along the Bar Lev line but then hesitated and switched to a defensive strategy when they might have maintained the offensive. The extent to which military or political considerations lay behind this tactic is yet unclear. But even a limited war with limited gains shattered the myth of the invincibility of the Israeli army and its intelligence apparatus. It also broke the myth of the fighting incapacity of Arab armies, and, most important of all, it broke the mood of fatalism and immobilism within the Arab world. But only temporarily, perhaps,

[1] See MERIP Repos, 'The October War', No. 22, published by the Middle East Research and Information Project, Cambridge, Mass., for an account of the politics of the October 1973 war.

[2] According to MERIP Reports, 22, ibid., under General Shazli some 50,000 students had been integrated in the Egyptian army's electronic arms section.

for Sadat's post-war tactics proved to be a logical continuation of the search of the Egyptian bourgeoisie and bureaucracy for close and amicable relations with the United States. The re-opening of diplomatic relations between Egypt and the United States was natural enough, as formal recognition that Egypt had handed Kissinger her negotiating brief in the dispute with Israel by then. Simultaneously, inside Egypt, the Sadat regime's domestic measures demonstrated that her diplomacy was part of a larger concern by Egypt's rulers to forge a close relationship with imperialist capital.

Western and other private capital was sought for the public sector. The most conservative oil-rich states were invited to invest. Some confiscated land was handed back to its former owners. The economy is to be 'liberalised' for private domestic capital, in harness with foreign capital. Libya's oil resources, accordingly, are no longer the most significant source of support on offer.

Perhaps more than anyone else in the Arab world, Gaddafi emerged as the loser of the 1973 war. Once Sadat and Feisal had been able to combine – and the history of the origins and sequence of this collaboration are as yet untold – Gaddafi and Libya were expendable. Saudi Arabia could offer infinitely more pressure with oil resources so much vaster than Libya's, and Saudi Arabia had excellent relations with the United States. The thrust of an Arab drive for the combined use of frontal war and the economic weapon of oil was provided by the Cairo-Riadh axis. Libya was left on the sidelines. When the fighting was over and a ceasefire in operation, Gadaffi was heard to be denouncing it as a comic-opera war, and accusing Sadat of a sell-out.[3] (The Palestinians had indeed been

---

[3] Gaddafi told Eric Rouleau of *Le Monde* on 23 October 1973: "This war is not my war. Sadat and Assad took their decision and worked out their plan without my consent, without consulting me, without even informing me. And yet our three countries are members of a federation whose constitution clearly states that war or peace could only be decided by a unanimous vote by the three presidents. I had once submitted to them a strategic plan, but their general staffs decided otherwise. I still think that my plan is better ... I'm in profound disagreement with Presidents Sadat and Assad even on the aims of their war. For me, the essential thing is not to take back from Israel the territories she conquered in 1967, but to free the Palestinians, all the Palestinians, from the Zionist yoke."

edged to the fringes of the event, to be kept there throughout the prolonged negotiations, for the war and its aftermath have less and less to do with the Palestinian issue.) Gadaffi refused to attend the Algiers summit in November 1973. He denounced Feisal as "nothing but an oil merchant". Relations between Egypt and Libya had rarely been worse. Passport controls were reimposed on Egyptians in Libya, and Egyptians there on official secondment were reported to be returning home.

· In this context, the Libyan-Tunisian merger proposal of January 1974 looked uncommonly like an act of pique on Gadaffi's part: overlooked by Arabs to the east, he would build a union with a country to the west. It was an enterprise even more precipitate and worse prepared than the proposal for union with Egypt had been. And it collapsed even more precipitately, reducing to the level of farce one more attempt to forge Arab unity from on high in presidential proclamation. Arab unity, said Tunisian opposition leader in exile Ahmed Ben Salah, "must not be used as a whiff of oxygen to save a regime already expiring."[4] He was referring to the internal state of Tunisia. As for Libya, every abortive unity attempt she tried was serving to discredit her own cause. The month after the Tunisian debacle, Gadaffi went to Egypt to patch up his differences with Sadat. His speeches were as obsessed with the need for unity as ever before ("If Egypt falls, then the entire Arab nation will collapse"). But by then, credibility in Gadaffi's capacity for sustained strategy was seriously strained. And, ironically enough, the Arab leader who had pressed hardest for the use of oil as a political weapon had been upstaged by oil-producing regimes that, until the war, had dragged their feet on every issue from Palestine to oil.

The effect of the war has been to isolate Gadaffi and Libya from Middle East political events, to strengthen the Sadat regime with its new-found allies, and also to rigidify the ruling groups in the most conservative Arab states which increasingly in the period after the 1973 war came to dominate events in the Middle East. For the war

---

[4] Ahmed Ben Salah, 'Le Peuple Tunisienen a Assez', *Afrique-Asie*, 48, 21 January 1974. See also *Afrique-Asie*, 49, 4 February 1974, 113. Salah (1926–2020) was a Tunisian politician and trade union leader.

which initiated the use of oil as a political weapon found not only Algeria and Libya ready to reduce production and place an embargo on shipments to Europe and the United States, but Kuwait, Iran and Saudi Arabia too.

In time – by March 1974 – the embargo imposed by the oil producers to pressure Europe and the United States to alter their policy on Israel was lifted. But by then, it was clear that the use of the embargo and production cutbacks during the war was part of a far larger crisis over the control of the world's oil resources and that oil was tilting the balance of world power.

The world's most advanced capitalist states, led by the United States, had to confront the fact that their economies' survival in the ensuing decade would depend on their oil imports from the Middle East, and this is precisely the period when the oil-producing states were threatening a cutback in production in a concerted policy to husband their oil resources. The embargo, which was, in any case, applied only partially, was nothing like as important as production levels. The Arab producers have begun to assert their power not only through their insistence on price rises but also by asserting their right to control production rates.

In the Arab oil world, the financial reserves of the producers have grown sufficiently large for their movements to affect world money markets and the fate of metropolitan currencies. Instead of investment by advanced capitalist economies in the underdeveloped, though wealthy, oil states, there is the prospect of the ruling classes of these underdeveloped states investing in the economies of the advanced capitalist world: a case of large-scale reverse-direction overseas investment.[5]

Arab oil money can, of course, be recycled back into the western economies through large-scale arms purchases and the import of high technology. Hence King Faisal's visit to Washington to call for United States aid to industrialise his country and negotiations between France and Libya. But even with the exchange of oil for western technology, the crisis of Western monopoly capitalism remains, for it is rooted in the declining power of the oil industry and receding western control

[5] *New Left Review*, p.1.

over the world's energy resources. From being client states of the West, the oil states are likely to become more assertive partners, forging in the process ever-closer links between western economies and policy-making and the ruling oligarchies of the wealthiest oil states, and yet at the same time deepening the contradictions between competitive capitalisms, both mature and emergent.

Hinged on the structure of the industry, the exploitation of oil has made Libya inescapably part of the international capitalist system. Though much of the economy is still blatantly precapitalist, the dominant mode of production is capitalist, linked to giant multinationals resting on American, British, and European monopoly capital and management. Despite its great wealth, Libya is dependent in the fullest sense of the word, providing crude oil to the metropolitan centres of the world in exchange for manufactured goods, foodstuffs, and even primary materials. Subordinated to international capital in the economy are the remnants of pre- or early-capitalist agrarian production, small-scale trading, an embryonic sector of the national capital in commerce and industry, and a growing state sector. The growth of the economy since oil has been phenomenal, but growth has been restricted to this highly capitalised sector and its direct subsidiaries on the one hand; and, on the other, to the public sector of the rentier economy's state, which is the direct beneficiary of the Libyan share of oil exploitation. Libya's series of confrontations with the oil companies are attempts to re-negotiate the terms by which the monopolies exploit the country's oil resources. The process is, as yet, incomplete. It is too soon to tell whether Libya can achieve more than partial control over the exploitation and use of these resources. For the meantime, then, between the multinationals and the state, there is thus both collaboration and yet a conflict of interests. On the surface, there is blazing hostility and a running quarrel over the pickings; but below this, there is a mutual dependence on oil and the cartel monopoly marketing structure, which, by its subsidies – in the shape of oil royalties – to the state, creates a large and constantly expanding public sector.

In an oil economy based on highly sophisticated technology more than in any other post-colonial state, there is thus illustrated not any classic contradiction between the interests of metropolitan bourgeoisies and an indigenous ruling class, but a fundamental source of collaboration. Hamza Alavi has demolished the concept of a 'national' bourgeoisie which is presumed to become increasingly anti-imperialist as it grows bigger so that its contradictions with imperialism sharpen.[6] This, he argues, is derived from an analysis of colonial and not post-colonial experience. In the post-colonial state, "the mutual relationship of the native bourgeoisie and the metropolitan bourgeoisie is no longer antagonistic; it is collaborative".

It is the nature of the post-colonial state which is crucial to an understanding of the role of Libya's army regime. The coup d'état is a recurring phenomenon in post-colonial societies on all the continents of the Third World, which are neither part of the advanced capitalist world nor socialist. The coup d'état brings to power a military-bureaucratic oligarchy which runs the country through its power over the state machine. The state apparatus in the post-colonial state is inherited from the withdrawing of – or ejecting – colonial power. And, in the nature of its pre-independence function, to institutionalise the subordinate relationship of the colonial population and society, it is overdeveloped. Yet it is, after independence, not the instrument of any single indigenous ruling class.[7]

In Libya, under the monarchy, the functions of the domestic state were controlled by a traditional oligarchy, linked with incipient elements of a new bourgeoisie under the direct tutelage of metropolitan power. The seizure of power was not so much a revolution made by the petite-bourgeoisie as one that has made way for its speedier formation. Under the Revolutionary Command Council, political power rests in a small army group that rules through its control of the state machine on behalf of a range of domestic social class interests, which are not identical but are mediated through the all-powerful and relatively autonomous

---

[6] Hamza Alavi, 'The State in Post-Colonial Societies: Bangladesh and Pakistan', *New Left Review*, 74, July-August 1972. See also Hamza Alavi, 'Bangladesh and the Crisis of Pakistan', *Socialist Register*, 1971, pp. 289–317.

[7] Alavi, ibid., pp.72-73.

state. Compared with post-colonial states in which there are competing interests between the indigenous bourgeoisie, landed classes, peasantry, the proletariat, and petite-bourgeoisie, Libya's social formation is relatively simple, and the state's role as mediator between the interests of conflicting groups, fairly uncomplicated. There is no policy against the development of an indigenous bourgeoisie, but the growth of this class has been and will continue to be limited by the state's economic ventures and control over the country's economic resources. There is no policy against acquiring private land, but no powerful entrenched landed class exists. There is a working class, but it is tiny, and its organisation and class action are government controlled. There is a great body of rural and urban poor, illiterate, sick, and under-employed, but one patronised by an oil-rich state which dispenses oil royalties as sheltered employment and welfare disbursements. There is a large and growing petite-bourgeoisie, mostly urban, ranging from small businessmen and shopkeepers to professionals, intellectuals, and students, and a huge spreading stratum of public officials. In new states, the advent of the petite-bourgeoisie is directly related to the increased numbers of officials in the state machine and the public sector. In an oil state, where massive resources are channelled directly to the state, the representatives of this bureaucracy manage the use of a handsome national surplus and its allocation. Under an army regime like Libya's, it is not the petit-bourgeoisie which rules directly – and a national bourgeoisie is virtually non-existent – but a military-bureaucratic faction that directly commands the power of the state. The army acts as a ruling class in charge of a statist economy.

In successive Arab countries (Egypt, Iraq, Syria, Sudan, and Libya), the petite bourgeoisie's closeness to power has run through young army officer movements. The army becomes not just the leading force of the petite-bourgeois revolution but one elevated above it and in control of it. The military in power is enormously self-confident; hostile towards autonomous political organisations, mass movements, and even civilian life as a whole. It mediates the interests of the petite bourgeoisie as its armed, organised, and most efficient representatives. Though it is not a class by virtue of its ownership of capital and means of production, it exercises the power of decisions over resources and the use of state capital. Most of these regimes have practised extensive Nationalisation measures and have built large public sectors of the economy. Nationalisation has generally arisen out of the struggle for independence in the economic as well as the political sense; in the absence of a dynamic and independent national bourgeoisie, this was one way of trying to give the economy a self-sufficient base. But when control was made no more accessible after the revolution to those strata of the population denied it before, economic power as much as political proceeded to accrue in the hands of a state which claimed to mediate the interests of all classes but which, in fact, was relatively autonomous of them all.

In contrast with the trained bureaucracy, the members of Libya's Revolutionary Command Council, the Free Officers and the ranks of the army are not generally recruited directly from the petite-bourgeoisie. They spring instead from the rural depressed in the interior and the under-employed or less established strata in the towns. But once in power, the army, and its subordinate partner, the bureaucracy, impose on the army, state, and populace the essential ideology of the petite bourgeoisie. This is in part because the development of the state apparatus and its allocation of formidable resources is accompanied by a massive rise in consumption, but also because the army-led revolution, in which the masses play no organised autonomous role, consciously adopts the ideology common to the petite bourgeoisie of the Arab world.

Because the petite-bourgeoisie is not a homogeneous class, but one that vacillates between the needs of small traders and farmers and petty officials, often close to the masses, and the interests of those higher up the social and employment pyramid-like larger landowners and businessmen, professionals, technicians, and the higher ranks of the administration, the ideology of the petit bourgeoisie is essentially wavering and pragmatic. It has constant shifts of emphasis, reflecting the shifting state of interests within this large, amorphous class. But it consistently seeks not to assert class interests within the society but to reconcile them. The 'non-exploiting bourgeoisie' is called upon to struggle for socialism like everyone else. The stress is on the need for an equilibrium between exploiters and exploited. The reconciliation of shifting interests is done under the aegis of the state and through state-initiated and state-run politics. Yet even the Arab Socialist Union is organised not as an alliance of class interests, united for the same objectives, but as a collection of individuals who have the right to express themselves as individuals but not as representatives of any class. Gadaffi is insistent that the Libyan Arab Socialist Union will not permit any manifestations of class struggle. Such is to be controlled by the state.

This leads to another characteristic of this ideology: a distrust of the masses and their autonomous action. The Baathist theoretician Michel Aflaq claimed that his movement represented, "the entire nation which is still in slumber, ignorant of its reality, unaware of its identity, forgetting its needs. We have preceded it, thereby represent it".[8] This is precisely Gadaffi's view of his own group's role in his country, and throughout the Arab world for that matter. This tutelage of the nation finds expression in the working methods and style of politics once these are allowed. Political instruments are created from the top; any existing ones are dissolved. The popular organisation is not for exercising popular power or initiative but as an instrument for mobilisation by the state and for gathering intelligence. The populist demagogy is passionate, but it disguises the manipulation of the people by the carefully fashioned instruments of the state.

The Arab nation, Gadaffi has said, dispenses with struggles for right or left on its territory. This is not to say that the state mediates as neutral or that all ideologies are equal. The rejection of any conception of the class structure of society and sources of conflict has led to a rejection of the independent role of dispossessed classes, whether workers or semi-peasants on the land or in the modern sector.

The search for a third way between capitalism and socialism and the rejection of the ideologies of these systems also leads

---

[8] Michel Aflaq (1910–1989) was a Syrian political theorist, journalist and politician who co-founded the Arab Baath Party.

to a search for more 'authentic' roots. Islamic socialism is the inevitable result for several reasons. In the first place, it expresses a genuine rejection of the impositions of the imperialist West. In the second place, religious doctrine already profoundly influences vast masses of people, especially in rural areas. And thirdly, the Islamic ethos preaches the equality of all believers regardless of wealth or occupation. Islam as an ideology and a set of rules for the organisation of social life inhibits the emergence of a class view. Islam also provides a language in which ritual and symbolic interactions either deliberately ignore the societal and economic structure or minimise its significance. Emphasis is laid instead on the value of belonging to a community, and the community is that of all believers.

Though Gadaffi's Libya abominates the organised right as much as the organised left, and the Muslim Brotherhood equally with Marxism, his own ideological compound of nationalism, religion, and social reform serves to clear the way for the Brotherhood's message, rather like John the Baptist did for Christ. The pull of religious brotherhood is invariably stronger in the countries which have been moved less by social revolution and class organisation. Libya is an ideal breeding ground for the belief of the Muslim Brothers and a source of inspiration to their counterparts in Egypt, regrouping visibly under Sadat's policy of conciliating the right and stirred by the political assertion of Islam by the reactionary states of the Arab world.

But whichever way Libya's internal politics shift, the political and economic mould in which she is cast as an oil rentier state with any army-run corporate political system, has set too hard for short-term political changes to alter that shape significantly.

Like their military counterparts in several other Third World countries, the Libyan military regime has ambitious plans to develop the economy as well as more means than most. But the development approach is characteristic of this style of statist, technocratic planning. The state actively intervenes in production and dominates it. Planning and execution are to be the responsibility of technicians and experts. The masses of people are to be beneficiaries of authoritarian paternalism; there *is* to be no participation or mobilisation from below.

The Mozambican Miners: A Study in the Export of Labour

The use of the colony of Mozambique as a labour reserve, exporting labour outside the territory where it fuelled centres of South African capital accumulation, is one of the dominant characteristics of the Portuguese colonisation of Mozambique in the late nineteenth and throughout the twentieth century. It is also a continuation of the dependent character of Portuguese colonialism and Portuguese capitalism throughout their history.

A detailed periodisation of Portugal's occupation of Mozambique has yet to be produced.[1] But it is clear that from the fifteenth century onwards, the activities of Portuguese mercantile capital, through the trade in gold, then in ivory, and then in slaves, were unable to fuel processes of primitive accumulation, which would consolidate a Portuguese capitalist social formation and a Portuguese metropolitan bourgeoisie. On the contrary, Portugal's

---

[1] These summary remarks on the periodisation of Portuguese colonialism in Mozambique are based on a seminar presentation to the Centro de Estudos Africanos (Centre for African Studies) during April 1977 by Nogueira da Costa and Luis de Brito. For the later period (see the following page) this material is based on a draft paper by Luis de Brito, 'O colonialismo português desde os finais do seculo ate 1930' ('Portuguese colonialism from the end of the century to 1930'). Work on the periodisation of Mozambican industrialisation: D. Wield, "Some Characteristics of the Mozambican Economy, Particularly Relating to Industrialization", Working Paper, Centro de Estudos Africanos. Maputo: UEM, 1977.

weakness within the world system and her subjection to unequal international competition blocked her transition from merchant to industrial capital.

Thus, in Mozambique, in the period 1785 to 1870, the Portuguese state had occupied itself with collecting customs duties along the coast and with the mono-export of slaves. By 1870, at the height of the imperialist power rivalry in Africa and the consolidation of British imperialism in the southern African region, Portugal could exploit her colonies only unevenly and by proxy.

Accordingly, in the period of the Chartered Companies, Portugal subcontracted her colonial exploitation in the north of Mozambique to British, French, German and other international capital. Under the system of Chartered Companies, the Portuguese government leased out a great part of Mozambique by granting concessions to private foreign capital to administer huge tracts of the colony. Thus the Nyassa Company, established in 1891 by largely German capital, had jurisdiction over an area of 190,000 km. The Mozambique Company, established in the same year by the British and French capital, controlled a concession of 155,000 km. And the Zambesi Company, established in 1892 by the French capital and others like the Société du Modal of 1904 and Britain's Sena Sugar Estates, constituted a significant sector of the colonial presence.

At home, the Portuguese economy was archaic and bankrupt. In the colonies, the shortage of Portuguese capital resulted in heavy reliance on British, European and, later, South African capital. This meant that the Portuguese colonial system lacked the capacity to valorise the economic and labour resources of the colony. In the past slaves had been used not for production but for sale as export commodities. The *prazos*, far from being agricultural estates, had, in fact, been installed to guarantee the circulation of commodities in regions crossed by trade routes.[2] So, too, with the turn of the nineteenth century, Portugal's more secure physical presence in the

---

[2] [Ed.] *Prazos* were feudal estates acquired by Portuguese colonialists and Goan traders and soldiers to exploit natural resources and formed the basis of Portuguese settlement and colonial expansion between the sixteenth and seventeenth century.

south – after the defeat in 1895 of the Gaza state – led in small part only to the organisation of forms of labour exploitation within the colony. The immediate response to the defeat of the rebellion of 1897 had been to profit from the export of labour, as this was the time of the establishment and rapid early growth of the South African mining industry. This dictated cooperation up to the hilt with the South African economy.

Beginning just before, but increasingly rapid after 1945, particularly in 1954, the Portuguese capital in Mozambique grew. This capital was dominated by the large monopoly groups which had come to exercise increasing influence over the Portuguese state. At the same time, these monopoly interests extended their presence, and yet they opened the colonies to a new phase in the entry of foreign capital. The period saw growing industrialisation, but it was industrialisation dominated by the export sector and one with emphasis on the consumption demands of a growing settler population.

Portugal's loss of ground in the Mozambican economy in the 1960s and the 1970s illuminated the two cardinal characteristics of the Mozambican economy, which have been consistent throughout the historical phases of Portuguese colonialism:

The continuing dependence on foreign capital.
The role of Mozambique as a service economy within the Southern African region: these services comprised the provision of railway and harbour facilities for exports and imports from South Africa and Rhodesia and, centrally, the function of Mozambique as a labour supply area.

The colonial structure of the Mozambican economy was accordingly the outcome of a double dependence. On the one hand, it was the product of dependence on a relatively backward capitalist economy constituted by the Portuguese colonial power. At the same time, it was subordinated to the needs of the Southern African economic complex. This latter integration became the predominant aspect of the structure of the Mozambican colonial economy increasingly.

The productive forces of Mozambique were shaped not according to the needs of capitalist development in Portugal but according to the needs of capitalist accumulation in Southern Africa. Portugal played the part of the rentier, deriving the major source of income from invisible trade and speculating on selling the labour-power of its African workforce.

A TWO-STATE SYSTEM

With the establishment of the gold mining industry on the Witwatersrand that labour export from Mozambique came to be organised on a huge and systematic scale. Before that, Mozambican labour had migrated to the Natal sugar plantations and the diamond fields of Kimberley, but this flow of labour had taken place before the Portuguese colonial state had established its hold over southern Mozambique – south, that is, of the River Sabi. The mining revolution in South Africa required heavy capital inputs as well as large and sustained supplies of cheap labour. Within South Africa, gold mining interests intervened actively in state policy to create a cheap controlled labour force from which rapid capital accumulation could be guaranteed. At the same time, the mining industry explored territories in Africa to its north, and even as far afield as China and other parts of Asia, in search of social formations where wage labour had not yet become generalised and where forms of cheap labour power could be derived.

Mozambique proved to be the critical labour supply area in the formative years of the gold mining industry. The foundations of that industry coincided with the defeat of Gugunyana in 1895, the subordination of the Gaza state, and the imposition over a large part of southern Mozambique, of a military government under which harsh and punitive measures were used to collect taxes and maintain colonial order.[3] Now the Portuguese colonial presence

[3] [Ed.] The kingdom of Gaza was initially established in Mozambique in the 1830s by Soshangane, the Ndwandwe general who fled from Zululand (eastern South Africa) after his defeat at the hands of the Zulu king Shaka. Ngungunyane, grandson of Soshangane, was the last ruler of the Gaza state, which held territory in what is now South Africa, Zimbabwe, and

could be extended beyond the leased areas of the north, beyond the trading posts of Inhambane and the fort of Lourenço Marques, and the way was open for the Portuguese administration to cooperate with South African mining interests to route labour to them and to profit from this trade in labour.[4]

This cooperation was institutionalised in state-to-state treaties for the sale of the labour force. The mining industry needed long-term and sustained arrangements to obtain cheap African labour. The Portuguese colonial state calculated on a continuing source of revenue and on assistance in building and maintaining the territory's infrastructure.

The Mozambican labour exodus to the mines was officially formalised for the first time in 1897. The *Regulamento* of that year constituted the first of a series of international agreements with the South African authorities.

The labour export had thus, since 1897, been formally organised and controlled by the two-state contracting parties. The Portuguese colonial government was guaranteed an income from the traffic in labour. This guaranteed income, in turn, gave the colonial state an enduring vested interest in continuing and enlarging the trade in labour.

It was the existence of vast catchment areas of tied labour which enabled the mining companies, operating through their monopolistic labour recruiting body, to force reductions in the wages of mine labourers in the early years of the industry, to undermine the resistance of African workers in South Africa to these reduced levels, and to maintain consistently low levels of wages over decades.

WHY MIGRANT LABOUR?

Over a prolonged period of time, then, Mozambique-generated

Mozambique. He led a rebellion against Portuguese rule in 1895 and was defeated.

[4] [Ed.] Lourenço Marques was the capital city under Portuguese colonial rule until independence in 1975 when it was renamed Maputo.

surplus in the shape of living labour, has been exported to the South African economy and accumulated there as capital. The process has produced the markedly uneven development characteristic of the Southern African sub-system.

In South Africa, the development of the mining industry – the cornerstone of South African capitalism – consisted of a rapid process of concentration and centralisation of capital. This capital was accumulated on the basis of a system of migrant labour drawn from the wider Southern African region. The early monopolisation of the mining industry created the conditions for the setting up of a carefully planned and institutionalised monopoly control of the recruitment of migrant labour. This monopoly was strengthened by state-to-state agreements with supplier states to guarantee the stability and continued reproduction of this labour force. Thus, the migrant labour system constituted and continues to be the foundation of capital accumulation in the mining industry.

We can, therefore, only fully grasp the particularity of South African capitalism by analysing the system of migrant labour, for this is the specific nature of the exploitation of labour power in this system.

A considerable literature now exists on the origins and development of South African capitalism, and as a central part, on the role and importance of migrant labour as the cornerstone of this particular form of accumulation of capital. It is not our purpose here to summarise or enter into this debate, but rather we shall attempt to present some of the essential arguments briefly as to why migrant labour constituted the source of the accumulation of capital in this industry.

As Marx has shown in his analysis of capital – the development of capitalism, in essence, consisted of the historical process of the creation of the proletariat. Thus, a class of people was created which is totally divorced from the means of production and left with no option but to turn their ability to work – their labour power – into a commodity to earn a living. To assure the continued reproduction of the working class, the value of labour-power has to be such that it allows not only for the reproduction of the worker's ability to work from day to day but also for the reproduction of his family (since his children constitute the future workers). Thus, in other words, the value of labour-power is determined by the value of the basic necessities which the worker and his family need to furnish present and future labour power. It follows that the surplus value appropriated by the capitalist is limited by the value produced by labour power on the one hand and the value of labour power on the other. Historically, the bourgeoisie has always attempted to reduce workers' wages below the value of labour-power and did so through excessive lengthening of the working day, heavy women's and child's labour, etc. But inevitably, such attempts came into contradiction with the necessity to reproduce the working class continuously. Only through reducing the value of labour-power itself, resulting from the increased productivity of the worker, could capital seek its expansion without threatening to deplete its life source.

The imperialist expansion of capital and its consequent integration of the oppressed nations in the international division of labour, shaped by the requirements of finance capital, relegated the production of cheap raw materials to the working masses of the oppressed nations. Thus, for example, South Africa became a centre of the gold mining industry within the international division of labour.

This industry required the formation of a working-class, with a very specific character. A system of migrant labour was created that distinguished itself from the working class of developed capitalist societies not primarily in that it migrates over long distances, but principally in that this class of workers never was completely divorced from its ownership of means of production. The migrant worker continued to own land and instruments of production, and hence continued to be able to produce part of his subsistence requirements as derived from these means of production. This allowed the capitalist producer to buy the labour-power of this worker-peasant below its value. As part of the subsistence requirements, of the worker and his family, continued to be produced out of his peasant base, which remained outside the sphere of capitalist production. Thus, precapitalist forms of production were made to subsidise capital accumulation by allowing the extraction of additional surplus value resulting from buying labour power below its value.

Obviously, such a system can only operate if the production, distribution and consumption process inherent in the precapitalist social formation is broken up in part to generate surplus labour to be provided in the form of migrant labour to the mines. This partial destruction of the precapitalist modes of production was initially achieved through the use of extra-economic coercive means such as the appropriation of better land and relegating the population to land reserves where the production base is insufficient (e.g. the S. A. Bantustan); the imposition of taxes; and forced labour as well as through economic means such as the destruction 'of indigenous crafts due to the importation of commodities (e.g. *capulanas* (African cotton cloth), hoes and other instruments of production).

The weakening of the economic base of the peasant society due to the extraction of labour-power from it, on the one hand, and the creation of new consumption habits on the other, gradually turned the migrant labour system into a system reproducing itself and one of economic necessity. Thus, as to the former, the changing division of labour between men and women in the peasant economy (the men being set free for wage labour), the reduced access to land in some instances, and the dependence on buying instruments of production as commodities, all these blocked the development of productive forces and made these communities dependent on income from migrant labour. As to the latter, new consumption habits of which the bourgeoisie consciously induced alcoholism to ensure a docile and addicted working class played no minor role, as well as the introduction of textiles and other consumer goods, which furthered the dependence on migrant labour income. Thus, the capital was accumulated on the basis of partially destroyed and partially reproduced precapitalist modes of production. The latter subsidised the former and therefore allowed for extra-surplus value to be extracted.[5]

---

[5] There is a good deal of literature on this process in South Africa itself and in other Southern African labour supply areas. Thus Colin Bundy in *The Emergence and Decline of a South African Peasantry* writes, "Much of South

In the previous section, we have tried to explain how, in the early development of capitalism in South Africa, based on the gold mining industry, labour drawn from precapitalist formations had been crucial to the rate of surplus value. These precapitalist societies were by no means only those within the geographical boundaries of the South African state, like the Transkei and other reserve areas. On the contrary, labour drawn from outside those boundaries has been a continually significant factor in the process of capitalist accumulation in South Africa.

The pattern of mine labour supplies over seventy-five years, from 1902 to 1977, demonstrates two distinct but related trends:

The differential proportions, within different periods, of South African and foreign labour and the change sources of foreign labour supply.
The remarkably stable and consistent character of the flow of Mozambican labour.

Historically, over half a century, there have been certain rises and falls in the supply of Mozambican and other foreign labour. These must be interpreted according to two different but related events. The first consists of the changes within the South African economy. On the whole, the more significant ebbs and flows of Mozambican mine labour relate to changes within the dominant economy of

Africa's history revolves about the transition of a majority of her people – the rural African population – from their pre-colonial existence as pastoralist-cultivators to their contemporary status: that of subsistence rural dwellers manifestly unable to support themselves by agriculture, and dependent for survival on wages earned in 'white' industrial regions and 'white arms,'" Bundy's study demonstrates the emergence of an African peasantry in about the 1890s in the Transkei, but then its decline within four decades. He writes "This process was a necessary component of . . . the process of capitalist development in South Africa," But this process led, in the case of the Transkei, to a rapid diminution in the productive capacity of the peasants. (Colin Bundy, "The emergence and decline of a South African peasantry." *African Affairs* 71, no. 285 (1972), pp. 369-388.

South Africa. At the same time, though to a lesser extent, the pattern of supply also relates to certain internal changes in Mozambique.

THE PROPOSITIONS OF SOUTH AFRICAN AND FOREIGN LABOUR

On the first issue, of the changing character of the South African mining industry within the South African economy, we are indebted to a penetrating new study which demonstrates how foreign labour has been consistently used to constitute the lowest-paid stratum of the South African economy's industrial reserve army.[6] The falls in size of Mozambican labour during the economic depression of the 1930s and again during the current recession of that economy show how Mozambican labour, like other foreign labour, has been retrenched in times of recession. The rises in the components of foreign labour and Mozambican labour, particularly in the 1950s, show that in times of boom, this labour is brought back onstream. This is a significant illustration of the point made earlier about the characteristics of the Mozambican service economy: that it is subject to the vacillation and crises of the dominating economy on which it was made dependent in the colonial period.

By contrast, from 1936 to 1951, there was a fall in absolute and relative terms in the numbers of South African workers in the mines. This was when there was not only an expansion in gold mining stimulated by the rise in prices of gold (the Free State mines were opened in this period) but also an expansion of manufacturing. At this time, there was an energetic expansion of foreign labour recruitment. By 1932 foreign labour constituted 43 per cent of the labour force; by 1936, it was 48 per cent; by 1939, it was 52 per cent; and by 1951, it was 65 per cent.

From 1951 to 1970, there was a rise in the total African labour force in the mines, and foreign labour recruiting was intensified and extended. Labour recruiting extended into parts of central Africa

---

[6] de Clercq, F., D. Hemson, D. Innes, and M. Legassick. "Capital Restructuring and the South African State: The case of foreign labour." In CSE Conference Paper, 1977.

not previously tapped for labour.

In this period, foreign labour was given preference over South African labour. At the same time, there was a rationalisation of the labour process in the mines. Certain training innovations for African labour were introduced, and a certain number of semi-skilled black operatives were created, especially in the new mines in the Orange Free State and Klerksdorp areas, which were more capital-intensive. From 1964 to 1972, the foreign labour component continued to mount until it rose from 64 per cent to 80 per cent of the total labour force.

It was after 1974 that the foreign labour component began to be heavily reduced. This is dealt with in the following chapters, which discuss changes within the mining industry and its effects on Mozambican labour in the post-1974 period.

THE ORGANISATION OF THE FLOW OF MOZAMBICAN LABOUR

The early period of the gold mining industry, from 1888 to 1913, was the period during which the Chamber of Mines, and its labour recruiting body, Wenela, created a sub-continental supply of cheap labour. What is striking is the strength and effectiveness of Wenela as a labour recruiting organisation. It was seen that it had the capacity to tap labour when it was needed and to turn off that supply with equal promptitude. The recruiting instructions to its network of Wenela stations were acted upon efficiently and rapidly. Besides a labour recruiting organisation of such power, government administrations were weak reeds. It initially took perhaps a decade for the system of labour recruitment to be well centralised, but when this was done, the organisation fulfilled its labour targets and rendered its complements of men to the mines with unfailing reliability.

Initially, when recruitment from Mozambique was not yet centralised, perhaps the greater part of the labour exodus across the border into the Transvaal had been clandestine. This labour movement had been heavily escalated by the measures invoked by the colonial government in the wake of the 1895 rebellion and the destruction of the Gaza state, and also by the rinderpest epidemic of 1896-1898 which decimated cattle herds in the southern provinces. Private recruiters and labour touts battened on the exodus and organised it. No detailed account has yet been written of the early recruitment methods, though recent research into Southern Mozambique describes how recruiting was conducted by 'runners'.[7] These worked for White or Asian recruiters and were employed to go from one settlement to another, seeking prospective recruits for the mines. The runners or recruiting police were identified by their red hats and some had a uniform resembling that worn by the administration police. They carried hippo hide whips. They received a per capita payment on their results. They carried safe conduct passes issued by the administration, though, in 1912, this system was ended because of complaints by Portuguese administrators that the coercive methods of these labour recruiters were abusing their authority. By then, *Negócios Indigenas* had been in operation for some years trying to meet the internal labour needs of *colonos* who could not pay wages competitive with those offered by the Rand mines, and on whose account the colonial state conscripted forced labour via the local administration and the chiefs.[8, 9]

But by 1912, when certain limitations were placed on the activities of runners and recruiters, the pattern of labour migration had been well-established. It had initially been induced by force, after the conquest of southern Mozambique and the depredations of the Portuguese colonial administration. In a fairly rapid period of time, the movement of labour had become self-reproducing. Rural producers no longer had any measure of real choice. They were either subjected to raids for forced labour or contracted to work across the border.

The absence of employment for Africans in southern Mozambique and the consequent 'attraction' of mine work is

---

[7] Young, Sherily, J., "Changes in Diet and Production in Southern Mozambique 1855-1960," British ASA Conference Paper, Durham, 1976.

[8] [Ed.] Negocios Indigenas refers to the rights and lifestyle of native africans of Mozambique. At the beggining of the twentieth century, Portugal was trying to establish legal limits to native population as a part of the colonial policy, so that the natives didn't have the same rights as the Portuguese.

[9] [Ed.] *Colonos* is the Portuguese word for colonizer.

graphically described in a 'Report on Native Labour Conditions' prepared for the Transvaal Chamber of Mines by one of its agents in 1922. In essence, this report argued, "no improvement in general conditions can be expected under the present system".[10] The report gave some instances of labour conditions, most of them drawn from the northern areas under the administration of the Chartered companies. But during 1921 and part of 1922 in the south, some 2000 natives were employed for months on the road between Xai-Xai and Xinavaan. All this labour was unpaid and barely fed.

In some cases, the natives even had to provide their own hoes, which cost about five shillings and were worn out in Government service. Throughout the whole province, roads had to be maintained in repair by the local natives without payment. And actually, other government service was also forced and unpaid in most Posts!

Before the Boer War, about 80,000 labourers or three-quarters of the total labour force in the mines were from Mozambique, and at that time, Mozambican workers were spending an average of three years underground, establishes that the industry was, in fact, virtually founded on Mozambican labour.[11]

After this initial period, the most striking characteristic of the continued flow of the Mozambican labour force has been the stability of supply and the consistency of numbers, especially from the late 1920s (after the signing of the Mozambique Convention).

A vast area of research remains to be done on the regulation of this labour supply, especially in the period between the two world wars when, with the exception of sudden dips in the depression years and a sharp rise to 107,000 in 1927 and 96,000 in 1929, the standing force of Mozambican labour stood at a more or less constant 80,000.

After the African mine strike of 1946, which was the most intense period of class struggle in the industry, foreign labour

---

[10] "Report on Native Labour Conditions in the Province of Mozambique," 1922, *South African Labour Bulletin*, July 1975.

[11] Transvaal Labour Commission, 1904, p. 4, 20, 28, 246. According to F. Wilson, "Labour in South African Gold Mines 1911-19621" from 1896-8 Mozambican labour constituted 60.2 per cent of the nine labour force, and in 1906, 65.4 per cent (p. 70).

comprised 59 per cent of the total African workforce, and the mines adopted a policy of trying to forestall further labour unrest by recruiting less completely proletarianised, that is, more foreign labour.[12] This is the period when foreign labour supplies were diversified. In the same period, Mozambique labour supplies rose.

CHANGES IN MINING IN THE 1970S

There is rather thorough documentation on the changes in the mining industry in the recent period, and the various factors which have contributed to these changes. These we summarise below:

Until the 1970s, gold mining was considered to be a declining asset. This was transformed by the international agreement to revalue gold at market prices. As a result, mining profits rose high, and there was a considerable increase in the value of funds available for accumulation and re-investment.

There had been a continuing decline in the South African complement of African mine workers. The dependence on foreign labour had increased. But this had occurred at a time of spectacular changes in the politics of Southern Africa, and changes which brought into question the continued survival of white minority exploitative regimes and, more immediately still, the degree of reliance which the mines could place on their regular contingents of foreign labour.

During 1973 there was a wave of African strikes, including ones in the mines and other forms of worker resistance. In 1973-5, in all 33 cases of worker resistance in the mines, some of which involved Mozambican miners. As Clarke has written:

These conflicts affected producer interests in two important ways: firstly, production levels dropped, and costs rose as confrontations spread; and secondly, a 'bleeding' of labour

---

[12] Legassick and Innes, Warwick Research Project study, see earlier reference.

supply took place as repatriation rose, strikers were dismissed, and disciplinary action and 'reallocation' were necessitated . . .. The industry was totally unprepared for these sudden and large-scale conflicts which were made all the more serious by the high gold price. Among a host of other factors, the conflagrations were strongly related to low wages, and the high degree of social control necessitated under compound conditions. The 1972-75 'wage reform', although begun before the compound violence escalated, would thus probably have, in any event, been necessary for some measure to restabilise the situation.[13]

Thus the rise in the price of gold and worker unrest made it possible and necessary to pay higher wages to African miners. Without higher wages, there was no possibility of drawing South African workers away from secondary industry and into mining – until the economic recession speeded the propulsion.

The production of a changed labour force was also closely connected with, and a result of increased mechanisation in the mines. While South Africa's deep mining technology is probably the most advanced in the world, it is an industry which is heavily labour-intensive, needing constant supplies of cheap African labour. As long as the price of gold was fixed, there was a tendency to rely on cheap labour and to move rather slowly towards increasing capital investment. This was not true, however, for all mines. While lower-grade ore and lower-productivity mines relied on cheap labour, newer, higher-productivity and more mechanised mines, principally those controlled by the Anglo-American Corporation, instituted higher levels of technology. Thus, as early as 1962, Anglo-Americans had broken with the labour policies of the Chamber of Mines and had urged higher wages to step up South African labour recruitment so that it could have a more stable labour

<hr>

[13] D. G. Clarke, "Contract Labour from Rhodesia to the South African Mines: A Study in the International Division of a Labour Reserve," Saldru Working Paper no. 6, Cape Town, 1976, pp. 11-12.

force among which it could institute a different wage structure on its higher productivity mines.

With the rise in gold prices, plans for mechanisation were accelerated. The paragraphs below describe some of the advances in mechanisation, for these have important effects on the quantity and the quality of the labour force as well as on the subsequent changes in labour recruiting and wage policy instituted by the industry.

MECHANISATION

Certain mechanisation had already shown effects in the mines by 1975. For instance, Goldfields Consolidated of South Africa Ltd. reported an increase of productivity of 11.5 per cent underground employee over 1974.[14] A mine belonging to Joint Consolidated Limited in 1975 had increased production despite a labour reduction of 20 per cent. This was done by introducing scrapers for loading the ore (instead of hand lashing), mono-rail cars, which required one worker rather than the two previously required, and mono-rope conveyors, used for carrying the mineral out of the mine. They were means to cut down unskilled labour near the mining, or stope, face. This was combined with more efficient management and maintenance systems, and by bringing white miners into management planning so that they could see the importance of working as a team and the role of their team leaders. Courses for training African aides to white craftsmen were begun, and some African miners have acquired skills in, among others, boilermaker, fitting, electrical work, and welding.[15]

The President of the Chamber of Mines, Mr A.W.S. Schumann, stated in 1975 that the total value of capital equipment used

---

[14] Formed in 1887 by British capitalists Cecil John Rhodes and Charles Rudd, Goldfields Consolidated was one of the first major corporations to dominate the South African mining industry, profiting from African labour and mines before becoming a major international mining financial house; *South African Mining and Engineering Journal*, November 1974, p. II.

[15] *South African Mining and Engineering Journal*, July 1975, and Mining Survey, April 1975.

underground by the gold mines was less than R250 million. He expected that equipment to the value of more than R1,000 million would be purchased during and as a result of the R150 million research programme over ten years.[16]

Much of the research and trials occur at or near the raining face (the stope face). "About 40 per cent of the Black labour force is employed there, and mechanisation is of great importance in reducing the Black labour force and improving productivity".[17]

It is these changes in the technology and the deployment of the workforce in the industry, together with increased worker militancy, and also, importantly, the South African economic recession which led to widespread African unemployment in that economy, which led to changed wage policies in the mines. There were changes in job grading and wage differential systems. This led to more African workers being categorised as semi-skilled.

In the period beginning with the 1950s and again in 1969, African wages had risen.[18] This was a period of chronic labour shortage but also of the beginnings of the rationalisation of the labour process and the introduction of training schemes for some African workers', especially in the more capital-intensive mines. But the wage rises in this period were considerably outstripped by the rises in the post-1973 period. By June 1976, the industry paid a minimum rate for underground work of R2.50 a shift.

The changes in wage rates immediately impacted the source of labour supplies. The number of South African workers in the mines rose rapidly. This was accompanied by an absolute fall-off in the numbers of contracted foreign workers, which trend is continuing.

It is clear that there were limits to the mechanisation of the industry. The new methods will seriously diminish, but they will not break the dependence of the mines on a large supply of African labour. But newer, richer, more capital-intensive mines will follow a distinctly different pattern from the older lower-grade ore mines.

---

[16] *South African Mining and Engineering Journal*, July 1975, p.31

[17] Ibid, 'Quote of Joint Consolidates head of Industrial Engineering Department', p.16

[18] *South African Mining and Engineering Journal* 1976, p. 17.

Within the work force, there will be the introduction of growing differentials in wages and skills.

Two of these factors will affect Mozambican mine labour in the immediate period:

The overall reduction in the use of foreign labour.
Differentiations within the African workforce and the reliability on more experienced and skilled workers.

These factors are reflected in the conditions of Mozambican labour after 1974.

ABOUT THE INTERNATIONAL UNION OF LEFT PUBLISHERS

Formed in 2020, the International Union of Left Publishers emerged as a platform for left publishers to promote left books on Red Books Day (21 February), to defend left authors, publishers, and bookshops, and to develop a copyleft method of sharing books across our countries and languages. There are approximately 30 publishers in our union.

Our previous joint books are *Lenin 150, Mariátegui, Che, Paris Commune 150, Kollontai 150*.

You can learn more about the IULP here: https://iulp.org/about.

The following publishers are producing an edition of *Selected Writings* by Ruth First: 1804 Books, Batalla de Ideas, Bharathi Puthakalayam, Editorial Caminos del Centro Martin Luther King, Chintha Publishers, Editorial El Colectivo, Editorial La Trinchera, Expressao Popular, Gono Prokash, Idea, Inkani Books, Instituto Simon BoHvar, International Publishers, Janashakti, Kriya, LeftWord Books, Marjin Kiri, Naked Punch, National Book Agency India, Nava Telangana, Ojas, Prajasakhti, Red Star Press, Tricontinental: Institute for Social Research, Vadell Hnos Editores, Vam Prakashan, Yordam Kitap, Zalozba /*cf.